D1160999

LUMMOX Press

A poet's muse can take many forms. Ann Curran finds inspiration in the personal stories and incidents of daily life. A journalism background informs her craft, but her stories would be hard to tell in a newspaper. It is her poetry that offers her the way to make sense of her world and ours. A native Pittsburgher, she finds much material locally, but, whatever the locale, her poetry is infused with humanity, wisdom, wit and grace.

—Reg Henry, nationally syndicated columnist
for the *Pittsburgh Post-Gazette.*

Pittsburgh is known for its quirkiness. Take the title of Curran's book. Yes, volunteers knitted blanket-sized squares to drape over the bridge. With a keen eye and boundless wit, Curran takes us on a wild ride through the streets of Pittsburgh and beyond, as well as along the trajectory of her Catholic school upbringing. One of my favorite poems is about a former student of hers, now a priest, who befuddles her when she tries to confess her "sorry old sins/ to a guy who just won't buy them." The poems in *Knitting the Andy Warhol Bridge* brim with heart, what we need in these confusing times.

—Nancy Scott, poet and managing editor of
U.S. 1 Worksheets

Happy 200th Birthday

to the

City of Pittsburgh

1816-2016

Knitting
the
Andy
Warhol
Bridge

Poems by Ann Curran

©2016 by Ann Curran

Cover design by RD Armstrong and Chris Yeseta, based
on a photo by Polly Mills Whitehorn and impressions of
Andy Warhol's Brooklyn Bridge Polaroid-silkscreen prints.
The back cover, photographed by the author, shows part
of a blanket crocheted by The Creative Hands at St. Paul's
United Methodist Church in Allison Park.

ISBN: 978-1-929878-62-8

Library of Congress Control Number: 2016930848

First edition

LUMMOX Press
PO Box 5301
San Pedro, CA 90733
www.lummoxpress.com

Printed in the United States of America

Contents

I. Tippy-Toe Touchdown, Hugs and Smacks

II. In Multiple Wakes and Places

Contents *(continued)*

III. Up on Mount Washington

IV. A Neighborhood of Make-Believe

Contents *(continued)*

V. "Cut Till You Bleed"

I
Tippy-Toe Touchdown, Hugs and Smacks

Inspiration to Perspiration

The day after the Super Bowl
testosterone floods the Y gym.
The guys are revved up beyond norm.
Flab flaps on treadmills. Sweat oozes
over bike seats. They heft weights greater
than their own in way too few lifts

to make any muscle notice.
Meanwhile, they watch endless reruns
of Tone Holmes' tippy-toe touchdown.
James Harrison hurdles himself
100 yards down the field again.
They don't show him bashing a Bird.
The boys would excuse his brashness.

The Ghost in the Sauna

I lie naked on the top shelf sucking up heat.
A black teen opens the door. She gasps and guffaws.

It's a ghost, she shouts to her classmates. I laugh, too.
Then the parade begins. They line up, shade their eyes,

look through the glass door at me, then run off giggling.
The bold and brave just whip the door open again,

wowed by this ghastly vision of total whiteness—
as pale as a white bra on a very dark girl.

Boxed Beach

The sauna is a beach without glare.
It's 130 degrees in there.

No sweat to attract wind-blown sand.
No boom boxes. No ocean grand.

No bodies prompting amazed gawks.
Just the quiet of a hot wooden box.

Wear a towel, flip-flops. Don't breathe deep.
Whatever you do, don't fall asleep.

The cedar captures, surrenders heat.
Solace for muscles, bones, if not feet.

The warmth is at least as hot as desire.
I leave when my toenails catch on fire.

Language Lesson

She carries her pink purse into the gym.
She insists she can't trust a locked locker.

On the treadmill, rivers run down her face.
She chuckles with Ellen on the TV

hanging from the Y ceiling to distract
exercisers. Then she pops the question:

Would you higher that TV for me, please?
Translation: Would you, please, raise the volume?

She believes that English is logical.
I higher it. Yes, she's blonde, but it's bleached.

Distractions at the PNC/Y

This bold Playboy pretty prances naked
in the ladies. Butt on high, she blow-dries
blonde locks. I suggest modesty. She spits
back a pissed, *Well, good morning to you, too.*
Now, she wraps herself in a towel but
blows her nose like a laryngitic tuba.

*

From the darkened sauna, I watch the teens.
They're so up, their feet barely touch the floor.
Yet they'll check their faces in my glass door.
One even turns to see her small behind.

*

In the gym, I count sets of bicep curls,
suddenly distracted by a guy's eyes:
intense, lagoon green, dark, curly lashes.
I don't take a second look. I would drown.

Winter Workout

Huge windows look out on Forbes Avenue
and Market Square—a better show than TV
on the treadmill with Stephen Colbert gone.

Wind plays with wraps around the half-built Hilton
swishing canvas and plastic out—sailboats
 against a sky-blue winter. Seven degrees.

Down below, cheek on street, a skilled workman
blows bolt holes in steel girders. Golden-orange sparks
splash the Fourth of July just for our eyes.

Enough fun. I try torso rotation.
Right: PPG's low-slung, mirrored spires reduce
Highmark to bunches of beige exam rooms
hiding such sad stories and costs from view.
Pittsburgh's glass castle lowers bulging snow clouds
as I pull down hefty sets of fifty pounds,
then head for the sauna's warm, dark sunshine.

Smell the Roses

The Y chalkboard asks for New Year's resolutions.

Jocks and weekend warriors reply:

Get a divorce

Lose 10 pounds by St. Paddy's Day

Drink more ~~beer~~ water

Stop drinking after work

Cuddle with my dogs and boyfriend

Complete two marathons

Bike 100 miles

Go to church more

Follow Jesus

Write on a random wall with chalk

Damp Drama

A Chinese woman teaches me
to take a hose, squirt the steam room
thermometer, unleash a mist

like Jack the Ripper's London streets.
Water drips from the door's lintel,
bubbles in rows on the ceiling,

explodes on bodies soaked in sweat,
floods the room, gurgles to the drain.
I almost hear the sharp clip-clop

of a dire horse-drawn carriage move
through the grey mist of Whitechapel.
There's nothing to fear here except

the bold Chinese woman who stands
astride a wet bench and stretches
to unscrew a wet, bare light bulb

so she can lie down, snatch a snooze
in this damp and cozy womb
that could suddenly turn tomb.

In Case of Emergency

I'll bash his privates and not break my toes.
Let's face it: I'm prepared for an attack

with a fierce self-defense course that showed me
how to kick with the upside of my foot.

Saturday morning, the Y women's room
fills with silence. No teens, hair dryers, chat.

I wash my hands and a tall guy appears.
I forget about screaming or running.

I glance at him in the mirror and say,
You're in the ladies room. He's *so sorry*

and beats a quick retreat. Stupid, I think.
What happened to my defense, my escape?

When I'm convinced that he has really gone,
I grab the emergency phone to tell my tale.

The Boy in the Mirror

He polishes the mirror wall
at the Y. He looks like most kids:
peaked cap, slight build, not bad looking.
Girls notice him. When he spies one
he freezes with a scary stare.
The girls and TV distract him.
He's a long time getting to work.

He sees the boy in the mirror.
They talk. Today, he hunkers down
low by the torso twist machine,
carries on a long chat session
with hand and facial expressions.
No one is there to answer him.
He doesn't show at the new Y.

At Fifth and Smithfield

Even old men in Depends eye up girls
with shorts so brief, they are beyond belief.

A mom falls asleep feeding her baby.
Methadone, a cop says. Helps her head home.

A drug-dealer girl insists on more cash.
The desperate buyer digs deep, finds green.

Black guys greet brothers with hugs and hand smacks.
Smokers are fearless out here on the street.

A slim drummer thumps out the daily beat,
a hollow sound at Mellon's empty bank.

Red Macy's has sales that stop Kaufmann's clock
and everyone shouts and they call it talk.

The tiniest of tykes walks by with fries.
McDonald's decides who lives and who dies.

A Theological Issue

Seen in heavy-duty, curlicued Gothic type
on a taxi-yellow T-shirt at the bus stop:
"When it rains, it pours,
but Jesus is our umbrella."

Is he a Totes, collapsed in hinged folds
and wrapped tighter than the consummate priss?

Is he a Monet waterlilies
or a Lily Pulitzer parasol

in island hues suffused with sunshine?
Or a great golf brolly, where a foursome

can huddle and head for the 19th hole?
And by the way, what would Jesus say?

Dump the bumbershoot and fetch the soap.
This is going to be one warm shower.

The Bus Flashes:
Never Forget 9/11/01 /39 Brookline

I feel like a radio lunatic
who insists we never went to the moon.
Neil Armstrong landed Apollo 11
at Meteor Crater in Arizona.

I gasped at 9/11 on TV.
I still can't believe this horror happened.
The planes strike, the people run. Disorder,
terror reign. Bodies tumble from great heights.
The towers collapse, people run again.
All planes down. In Pittsburgh military
aircraft fly on, stunned by Flight 93
down with no survivors near Shanksville.
All more unbelievable than a moonwalk,
more unbelievable than a baffled Bush.

Life Walks by at the Corner

Barefoot babies in strollers flex
their feet to stop its fierce onslaught.

The green wigged guy with horns on head
switches phones into cameras.

The homeless vet sells tiny flags
too small to bleed, cry and die for.

Little black girls forget their hair,
plaited cornrows and colored beads.

Port Authority police park
across the street and watch for sales.

When their bus comes, most are relieved
to head for their version of home.

Business at the Bus Stop

She looks like a suburban Mom
at the bus stop with her small kid.

Three security guys zoom in
on her, search her purse and wallet.

The daughter doesn't seem surprised.
Regulars at the stop whisper,

She tried to sell some of her pills.
She stays cool. The cops go away.

The crafty know you don't ever
sell to strangers. It's bad business.

Ground from the Rumor Mill

The flower guy, parked between Saks
and McDonald's, got arrested.

He tried to help the fuss-budget
who wanted *Something exciting.*

Not a daisy, lily or rose.
Something that will grab attention.

He hadn't a bit of patience.
Her verb nudged him. He grabbed her ass.

Parolee Patter

She says:
I tried to kill myself.
Set the damn house on fire.
Did four years, 30 days.

He says:
Shit, I missed so much school
when I was in jail, they
said I couldn't come back.

She has no upper teeth.
He wears no winter coat.
She couldn't be thirty.
He's a high school kid.

They talk as fierce winds strike
the shrinking city.
Both board the same bus
heading to the same place.

When Kaufmann's Clock Stopped

Call it Macy's all you like.
Word over the door tells all:

    Kaufmann's

carved with depth in a grand size
to outlive some little guy.

Lions above glare with rage
at the unwashed, unwelcomed.

Cherubs with stone horns proclaim
the storekeeper's great grandeur.

Cream-colored ceramic tiles,
curlicues encase this pile

that once lit up the dark town.
Walk softly, friends. It's a tomb.

Riding the Bus with Billy Collins

We cross the river, cut through the tunnel.
He putzes around his place, saves a bird
caught inside, pads barefoot through damp grass
to catch another morning breaking through.

The driver beep-beeps the stairs down
for a grocery-laden senior. Billy
traces the Elk River to its demise.
At every stop an old man or woman

mounts the bus on the way to a cheap lunch,
cards, cracking jokes at the Senior Center.
Billy stays awake all night in deep fright
over turning fifty. His backyard lake

calms him. He hates that students tie poems
to a chair, beat the meaning out of them.
His prep for writing: clean your desk, your house,
clean *the undersides of rocks*. Get the dirt!

II
In Multiple Wakes and Places

Shipwrecked Survivors

With lunch on my lap at the Lawrence Center
I see summer's face on the Allegheny.

Neon-yellow kayaks spin paddles
and flip water to the skies.

Three slick, white runabouts raise waves,
make an ocean of this green river.

Bikers vanish behind trees on the far shore.
Once, we rode bikes on the graffitied Jail Trail,

across the Hot Metal Bridge to the South Side,
swinging by the Steelers practice place,

near orthopedist Freddie Fu's limping landmark
where my left ACL was pronounced dead.

Up the Allegheny with our boat, Der Taob,
we're stuck on a sandbar—shipwrecked survivors.

Water shallow enough for you to get out
and push our craft back into a river float.

Then down at The Point in dark after
a booming fireworks display,

dozens of boats argue with the rivers' currents,
bounce about in multiple wakes.

Then POW! Getting hit by a big, boozy yacht
that shot off into the night, not knowing if we'd tip.

With instinct, I reach beyond you
for the life jacket somewhere on the wet deck.

Catching the Blues

Once I went to sea
in a Jersey tub
that bobbed in the waves
like a drunken cork,

spied on fish beneath.
We chugged for minutes
then dropped all our lines.
I pulled in six sad,

squirming, dying blues
watched their quick gutting
refused to claim mine.
Leaned over the side

to spit out my gum
and without a thought
gave the survivors
my breakfast and lunch.

Not Blue

In the paint store she told the guy
she wanted gray with green. Not blue.

His words stopped making sense to her.
She got in her car. Then, nothing.

When she awoke she was confused.
Darkness had descended too soon.

She didn't recognize the signs.
She headed home. Gave us a call.

Pull off the road, we urged her
not knowing if the seizure had come

or was about to black her out.
I'm at the red light near the bridge.

I just want to go home. I'm close.
We curbed our hysteria.

No. Go straight to the hospital.
It's closer. Left to the ER.

She listened this time. I recalled
the skiff on a lake in Canada.

She'd refused to paddle with me.
A storm rumbled, grumbled down the dark.

Park by the door. Tell them seizure.
Silence. *They're helping me.* Sweet words.

Those Purple Things

What are those purple things on the houses?
I ask my teacher about my photo
shot from the bridge across Panther Hollow.
Shadows, he says. *They always turn purple.*

A corner of the humidifier,
slurping water from the basement air,
turned blue. Blue as San Diego's ocean.
Blue as Bugleweed blooming in July.

Blue as my husband's eyes: yes, old, not new
not borrowed, just blue. I walked the longest
aisle in town, six pence shuffling in my shoe,
superstition gliding to the altar.

Photos, black and white. No purple. No blue.

River Quiver

The sun sits on top of Mount Washington.
The river takes its picture near the wharf.

A circle of half-crazed light jiggles, jumps
like subatomic particles, sparkling,

skipping loosey-goosey with pure delight.
Yet, it reins in that wet quivering shape.

The sun dips, moving the circle downstream.
It multiplies through the P & LE sign.

Six suns appear twitching, frenzied. They guide
the Mon as it weds the Allegheny.

Crossing Over

A bridge is as close as most come
to walking on water.
It goes from here to there. Sometimes
makes all the difference in the world.

I Like a Day

when the bridge lies on its side
in the river. When slim nymphs,
dressed in a few flowers, dance
on one building and reflect
in panes across the alley.
When my shadow stretches down
the sidewalk and colors show
their richest hues. When the sun
beams off Highmark's rocket top
with blinding blaze, and folks fill
treadmills, bikes, ellipticals
trying to buy fifteen more minutes
on this spinning sphere in space.

Knitting the Andy Warhol Bridge:
Art Becomes Blankets for the Homeless

Andy Warhol's small Carpatho-Rusyn mother
might have gathered like this with her New York cronies
to gab and giggle about Andy, his projects
and what their old men think of her shy pop artist.
Talent flows through these knitters' fingers, shades, designs.
They cover the tall railings of the Warhol Bridge

not far from brother Paul Warhola's scrap metal yard.
They think Paul was smart becoming an artist, too.
Some loop troopers make tight blocks of magic. Green buds
on a blood red background. Others so disjointed.
The gleaming blue of river seeps through yarn windows.
Pink, purple, teal pieces blend with colors behind.

A pattern pulls like a blanket in a shared bed.
These busy artists resort to canned soup for lunch.
Their needles, hands, thoughts demand beauty, order, peace,
and they send it dancing across the Warhol Bridge.
A homeless Marine on sidewalk seat asks for change.
First in line to cover cold with this knitted warmth.

Frozen River Myths

Last winter, Gram's crazy story came true.
Pittsburgh morphed into Minneapolis.

The three rivers froze. A couple of cops
chased a thief over the Allegheny.

Those little tugs pushing tons of barges
on the Monongahela and Ohio

chomped through the ice like T-Rex at lunch time.
An open channel formed a small river

to carry tons of black gold to burn downstream.
Up on Mount Washington my fingers blanched.

The zoo closed, locked the polar bears inside.
At sub-zero, schools delayed two hours.

Me? I'm a born chicken at heart, but claim
I'd like to dance all the way across—next time.

Occupational Hazards

When your family includes a Navy SEAL
phone calls at strange hours terrify you.

Never knowing where he is, what insane
undertaking he's involved with, you see

him scramble through the dark of some country
you never heard of to save some people

clearly and forever our enemies.
Or he swims with buddies at night beside

a cliff they'll climb to kill someone pleasant
who wants nuclear weapons just like ours.

And that kid, still a kid, walking around
with blood on his hands, in his heart and head.

So you think about that Christmas when he
guarded the Obamas in Hawaii.

And you feel proud and slightly less frightened.

On Washing the American Flag

It flapped out front from Memorial Day
to July Fourth and beyond. I love
to see it waving, hear the click-click
of metal holding it against the pole.
But frankly, my dear, it's filthy. Time
to submerge nylon in Ivory Flakes.
One star winks as whites brighten. The red
as red as fallen troops' blood in battle
or collateral damage. It's coming clean,
but something grew along the band that holds
it all together: Spots I can't remove.

I wonder if we can ever clean it.
Wash out the stains that flag-waving hides.
Reservations that continue the wrongs
against the first native Americans.
Racial hatred passed on like DNA
from parents and teachers to children.
Little Boy and Fat Man vaporizing
Japanese boys, girls, men, women.
The first non-WASP president shot in the head.
A black man who dared to dream brought down.
My Lai, Abu Ghraib, Guantanamo
uncovered a U.S. I don't know.
Oh, why wear it on your lapel. Its dreams
have gone to hell. I hang it out to dry.
A bird craps on it as it passes by.

Just a Big, Yellow Duck
Anchored on the Allegheny River

Hundreds of nursery school kids
hand-linked, jerked like paper cutouts,
stare bewildered at the mammoth
forty-foot high Rubber Ducky.
Thirty-feet wide it dwarfs real ducks
splashing about below its bod.
Black eyes, white pupils see nothing.
Odd orange mouth is sealed and silent.
A serious piece of art
by Dutch Florentijn Hofman,
known for a Big Yellow Rabbit
in Sweden, beached Grand Pianos,
giant Crow in the Netherlands,
a Fat Monkey in Sao Paulo:
world's largest urban installations.

Inflatable Images built
the duck somewhere in Ohio.
A million came even in rain,
armed with cell and real cameras
charmed by this shiny, plastic sun.

On Glacier Bay

The glaciers star today.
We celebrate their coming

with Dutch pea soup on deck.
We stretch out on lounge chairs,

cover up with woolen plaids.
We wait. And wait. And wait.

The liquor guy rolls by.
At last, when we've gone to lunch

the big glacier looms on port
or perhaps it's starboard.

No, wait, the ship turns. It's both!
White wall, streaks of black debris.

Blue of ice wrung almost dry.
Green bounces off mountain moss.

We float gently on the bay
birthed by this great white giant.

The Laundry Line

The Gold Rush made a wild west of Alaska.
Fort Seward became an answer to discord.
Officers lived in Victorian mansions
at the top of Haines. A parade green out front.
A step down, the wives of Army non-coms
washed the officers' clothes in Soapsuds Alley.

On Tour in the Great Land

The train chugs by millions of spruce stunted
by permafrost into slim pencil trees.
We pan for tiny specks of gold, encase
them in 14K and see-through plastic
in the dim company store, an escape
from the slant of Alaska's summer sun.

*

High atop a stern-wheeler we look down
on an Iditarod farm. Barking dogs,
each with its own house, leap to the roof, jump
off, begging to get picked for a trial race.
They take off like a final Indy lap:
around a pond, through the woods and back.
Puppies imitate them mounting a log.
The trainer gives them a butt-boost over.
It only pays in glory, mushers say.

*

Throngs of excited tourists filter off
the wooden boat into a reproduced
Athabaskan village hung with fur pelts.
A native girl with grandma stories tells
us how life was in the cold, olden days
before she went to the university.
Fur traders came. The U.S. bought the state,
larger than all forty-eight other stars
with its Aleut-orphan-designed flag
of the Great Bear and North Star on blue sky
dangling in the nation's cleanest air.

*

A bus carries us to the great pipeline
raised in spots to allow moose to cross under.
It came with its own highway and workers
standing by to unplug any problems.
The pipeline drained Prudhoe Bay of oil.
Now Alaska looks for more places to suck
black gold into its shiny silver snake.

Last Stop: Ketchikan

The rains come to Ketchikan when we dock.
Tourists finally don their must-have ponchos.
They focus on the totem poles inside
and out, native art in Scanlon's, colored

with the intense shades of Alaskan
flowers saturated with hours of sun.
Some hit the jewelers hungry for gems:
blue diamonds, black coral, tanzanite, emeralds.

Others head for the creek shop souvenirs,
escape from the downpour in this rain forest.
They abandon the shops and salmon samples
to rush to the angry creek. A sea otter

snatched a salmon. *It got away*, they say.
Cameras snap. *No, he's caught it again.*
Some pulled for the fish; others, the otter.
Some saw themselves in this same damp battle.

In Siberia

they train great brown grizzlies
to stand on their hind legs
wearing ice skates,
kneepads, face masks.
The bears smack the puck
with the anger of people.
Sometimes they hold the stick
upside down.

When a bear misses the goal
he roars through the mask,
clouding the cold air
around the muzzle
that stops him from tearing
his opponents apart.

The people in Siberia
shout at the bears:
Kill! Kill! Kill!*
Their voices steam
the chilled air of the arena.

*Translated from Russian
to ease the readers' way.

I Ran Where Ancient Women Never Walked

When I arrive at the Olympic field,
the pillars lie like fallen dominoes.

Wildfires still glow in trees beside the site.
The forty-foot gold and ivory Zeus

had exited, thoroughly disgusted
by gross cheating at the very first games.

The field looks piece-of-cake easy. I run
with a world marathon junkie on grounds

where ancient women could not even walk.
Some athletes wore loin clothes till one lost his

and won. Next time, they all chose birthday suits.

*

On Patmos Island, John the Divine,
banished because he preached about Jesus,

holed up in a dank cave. The ceiling split
in three, opened to *The Apocalypse*—

how it would all one day come to an end
and we still wouldn't understand his book.

He listened all night and wrote in the light.
Still wore a deep groove in his rock pillow.

In Botswana

When they run in a herd
across the Kalahari
they become grace floating.

When they nibble treetops
they stand taller than all
other living animals.

When their hearts pump blood
all the way to their brains
it's a clear miracle.

When they meet sharp objects
their skin refuses to tear—
a model for space clothing.

When they're old and descend
too deep in a water hole
they die trying to get out.

At Cogan Station in Upstate New York

At Jack & Sarah's Family Restaurant
that looks like an expanded roadside diner
with cutout hearts, wise plaques, flag-waving decor,
a zealous, happy Sunday crowd scarfs down
bacon, eggs, sausage gravy on a muffin—

a tasty pig-out. A waitress pulls up a chair
at our table with the warmth and concern
of a physician's assistant. She's eager
to prepare our veggie choice minus oil.
Fat free dressing? Nope. *How about a lemon?*

Green beans? Sorry, we cook them with diced ham.
Want a nice (but naked) *baked potato?*
It's touching. Such kindness from a hot spot
where veins get clogged daily for folks who long
for splurting oil, a side of sweet potato fries.

Along The Strip

I can't visit the Heinz History Center
without thinking of that future president
done in by a plane-helicopter crash.
All that promise dropped in flames to the ground.

When I park in the lot across the street
I wonder what year I might bike trails
 on both sides of the Allegheny River
or if business will grab that land again.

If I stop at St. Stanislaus or see
St. Patrick's knee-bending, fanatic stairs
I always recall Father Nichols, banned
to The Strip, blind to his crooked bookkeeper.

Chatting in Pamela's pancake place
with old Sacred Heart girls, we remember
the kindness of Charity nuns who saved
our lives and led us down so many paths.

Driving by all those thin ballerinas
up Liberty Ave., I hope and pray they
find dance work that will allow them to eat
and prepare for what life does to bodies.

At the craft gallery, I hear again
Joseph, as deaf as Beethoven, reading
his poetry with angles and rhythms
that slide sideways like a car spins on ice.

I can't return a dead-eyed stare to fish
in Wholey's Market and still order up
a Nola gumbo and a Wholey Whaler,
1 lb. whiting fish sandwich, I should share.

At Kaya's Caribbean restaurant
I pop down luscious lentil /corn beignets,
conch chowder with sweet potatoes, pepper
and a jerked, but not jerking, grilled swordfish.

Singing Sand Dunes in Morocco, Oman, Chile

Researchers at Diderot University
in Paris say some sand dunes sing in a low, droning pitch.

If the sand dunes sing, as some say—
even Marco Polo in his day—

why not the sea against the rock,
music to some around-the-clock.

Why not the continents afloat,
groaning, growling a long bass note?

Why not the Earth spinning in space
hardly soundless without a trace?

Why not the planets' whimper-pang,
still stuttering from the big bang.

Give scholars a grant, and they'll explore
most puzzles you leave at their door.

Blame the wind for the sand dunes' song.
It's shoved grain against grain all along.

III
Up on
Mount Washington

Eds-and-Meds City from on High

People come to Mount Washington to see Pittsburgh.
They speed up McArdle or crowd into inclines
to walk Grandview, day and night, gasp at our town.

The muddy Mon blends with the green Allegheny
to swell into the wide Ohio by Heinz Field,
just a few blocks from PNC Park, both proposed

by Sophie Masloff, the city's first female
and first Jewish mayor, who almost got laughed out
of office for suggesting two stadiums.

The fountain at Point Park rises fifteen stories
shrinks to a toy from the hilltop.

Bridges span the rivers connecting neighborhoods
to downtown lying in a parenthesis between universities.

On winter nights you see a sliver of PPG's Christmas tree,
the fairy tale turrets of the tall glass castle,
watch music moving ice skaters around the rink.

Me? I Go Up to Grandview to See the Clouds

I leave my brick quarter of a building
where our oaks and elms block the wide blue sky

here on the back of Mount Washington—
where trees get care like your pampered poodle.

Placed in space, I'm eye-level with the clouds.
In summer they rise higher than skyscrapers.

Tiny planes emerge from one, enter another.
Limos deliver crowds of brides to overlooks

where they pose with parties at the top of their world,
arrive late at the biggest event of their lives.

It reminds me of Gram who had no real wedding.
Just a rectory quick fix before the baby's birth.

First Date

He took me to Phil's*
on Mount Washington.
Cheap drinks, peanut shells
on the floor, *Duck Soup*
on the screen. Told me
I didn't have to
make him laugh. Relieved
I married the guy.
We still laugh a lot.

*Now upgraded to Bigham Tavern

I Got Married Anyway

I thought I would have a dozen children
and I got married anyway.
I said I wanted to be a writer
and I got married anyway.
The Pittsburgh Catholic newspaper fired me
and I got married anyway.
The boss found me another job, part-time,
and I got married anyway.
My eggs refused to bloom into babies
and life began to change for us.

I fell in love with Ireland and the past.
I grew into a kind, crazier bitch.
I wrote in ways the world would reward.
I learned that friends, work can fill much of life.

After a decade, a woman gave us
the sweetest, green-eyed, blonde baby daughter.
She made all the difference in our marriage.
We found there was someone we would die for
and as we died, I became a writer
and learned mothers work at home *and* outside,
that daughters are the joy of fathers' lives,
that those who give to others will receive
more than they could imagine or believe.

One Cool Cat

His Nicholas Mosse mixing bowl
circles in the microwave

like a cat easing into a nap.
The cereal bowl proved too small

for his morning dish of oatmeal
which puts him to sleep on the couch,

mouth open to snap at daydreams.
I wish he could count on nine lives.

Greedy, I'd want in on those, too—
sheep farmer in Dunquin, Ireland

to banned-book printer in Shanghai.
Oops! Eternal life slipped my mind

Night Prayer

For the primrose abloom
with gold center that yields
to apricot petals
thriving on the kitchen sink
even in winter's pale sun.

For the window of blue sky
that brings back the rushing sea,
sand scattered on cool tiles
warm bodies tasting of salt.

For this husband of mine
as we nestle like old dogs
my head lifted by his lungs
a tangle of limbs:
Which are mine?
Which are his?

The Grand Finale

Bless Zambellis who shoot them off,
the Nuzzos who invite strangers

into their narrow, dark side yard
that opens to the three rivers

below our Mount Washington perch.
Boats stop behind the flashing buoys

safe from the pyrotechnic barge.
Then the beauty and noise begins—

in the water, mid-height, on high—
gold, pink, white burst in our faces.

Co-joined circles, darts of light, stars.
Such power from a slim, black barge.

Fireworks mark the country's birthday
while we debate a period,

or misplaced, missing period,
in our famous Declaration.

Then the grand finale explodes—
rockets, lights, sound blasts everywhere.

The thrill is tinged with sudden fear—
the old, familiar sound of war.

Keeping Order at Chatham Village

I live in the Garden of Eden.
No apple bans here, no apple trees either.
But eighty-plus years of rules keep us in check.

No signs: political or otherwise.
No grills on porches or balconies.
No Big Wheels before 9:30 a.m.
or after 6 p.m. Three-pet limit inside.
They make an exception for fish of course.
No dogs, not even visiting dogs.
But, get a letter from your psychologist.
The night watchman said of our visiting
corgi: *That's sure a healthy looking cat!*

But if you know the rules, you also know
there is nobody in our two hundred homes
who isn't breaking one or more of them.

Beset by Bats and Bees

The bats had shat once too often
on the fake purple irises
thriving in a loose-knit basket
on a sunless patch of front porch.

Who knew the bees snuggled down
beneath those silk flowers and faux
soil, beneath green styrofoam,
constructing a beige honeycomb?

Suddenly evicted, one buzzed
anger all afternoon. Baffled
as it repeated searches of
the right spot for its vanished hive.

At the Playground

In my neighborhood,
maybe in yours, too,
young couples, partners
don't plan play sessions

for their preschoolers.
They get together
in our small playground
with their indulged dogs

who used to poop and pee
on the playing fields.
A politician
fenced off the sled run

for the four-legged
babies so parents
can meet, chat and brag
in their doggie space.

Moonstruck

It's 8 a.m. and a full moon shows its face
above the blush on top of the maple tree.
Floating in a sea-blue sky, somehow
it's forgotten to set. I'm so distracted
by this distant sphere, I catch the wrong bus,

hustle along Grandview Avenue to find
the right one. Along the way I pick up
a stray penny and a D.A.R.E. button
urging me to resist drugs, violence,
booze, marijuana, things that make you fly.

No mention of the moon tugging me
wingless into the blue. No mention
of the moon pulling me from my daily
routine. No mention of the moon refusing
to run away with the beautiful dark night.

Squawk Talking

Once a year the crows appear
in quiet Chatham Village.

Such screeching. Such squawk talking
like nine hundred loud women

having brunch, watching fashions,
buying basics from boutiques.

These black birds line bare branches,
swoop overhead. Cry! Reply!

Shriek orders to each other
until you expect Hitchcock

of the pregnant paunch to cue
an attack of killer birds.

The Blessings of Rain

The hedge wears a pale halo of new growth
prompted by one day's incessant rainfall.

It sent Saw Mill Run seeking higher ground
washing across 51 and 88.

It forces the newbies on Mount Washington
to find alternate exits from the heights.

When the rain stops, the earth smells bathtub fresh.
Leaves gleam. Bits of blue sky float in puddles.

ANN CURRAN

The New Pastor

For Father Michael Stumpf
St. Mary of the Mount Church

He wears sandals like Christ and Franciscans
who walked through his childhood, showed him the path.
He rides bikes and loves to go to the beach.
Wears a wedding band, protection perhaps,
from hot chicks crazy not to come on to
a slim, summer-blond guy with unstoppable smile.

He's thirty-four, merely a baby priest.
Not afraid to say he sins, forgets prayers
for days at a time, urges the faithful
to open their hearts to different people:
the food co-op kid with rings in his nose,
lips and eyebrows, the Latino next door,
college students with raucous beer parties,
even the half-black U.S. president.

Put down the iPod, the Wi-Fi-fed notebook.
See the live people in your family,
your office, your bus, he says. Deal with the real.
I pray he will not run away with the cute
youth leader, some fresh-faced nun, or the pert
organist, the cool, gifted musician
his garage-band soul once wanted to be.

Morning Show

The mullioned windowpanes project
a black and white show on the wall.

Small screens hold a single oak leaf,
sprigs of spring, two crisscrossed branches.

When the wind blows, vertical streaks
of gray and white shimmer across

the screens like early TV snow.
When it rustles, they lift and sigh.

Like ghosts of the everyday world,
they flitter, drift and disappear.

When the Paper Guy Sleeps In

There I am in the gingko tree
like one of the visiting squirrels.

I'm curled in my fluffy, pink robe
blowing my ever-running nose.

Light plays such tricks in this kitchen.
My neighbor's upstairs window hangs

with my sister's stained glass red heart
deep in the microwave's innards.

A bathroom leak echoes the heart shape.
The stove becomes a snowy walk

on the side of my oatmeal pot
for a huge, harmless, black spider.

The paper guy is sleeping in.
On the fridge, the Acropolis,

a tall Amsterdam house nuzzle
close to President Obama

having a beer in Moneygall.
Not a squirrel climbs the ancient tree.

Only falling acorns or sex
arouse them from their comfy nests.

The Plane Truth

The London Planes shuck off their skins
like snakes. I crush them underfoot.
These accidental hybrids grew
in seventeenth century Spain
when an Oriental Plane tree
and an American Plane stood
within shooting distance and tossed
eager seed balls at each other.

An errant barefoot maid dallying
in the garden with her master
pressed the seed to soil and sparked
this urban wonder that withstands
disease, sheds its gray, olive brown
bark and, standing pale and naked
in the world, arms raised on high
in question, shows off its winter coat.

An Old Story

One day, the guy who guards the gardens
figured out how to let the sun shine

on everyone's little, private plot
jammed between the tennis court and woods.

He meant no harm, tired of the complaints
from flower, spice and veggie planters.

Something made him take action that day.
He girdled the tallest, fullest trees

preventing nourishment from rising.
It was slow irreversible death.

No one, no one was happy with him.
He was surprised at that, the big fine,

and getting banished from the garden.

Earth's Oldest Tree

The gingko does not give up its gold easily.
Thousands of mini-suns ride the wind, fling their fire,

refuse to let go and join the universal fall.
Great jumping piles of maple and elm leaves muddy

the grass. The dogwoods bleed their loss in cherry red
while the gingko sways curved branches, ripples lemon fans,

holds all the gaiety of summer past against
rugged, life-carved bark, older than the dinosaurs.

When the Polar Vortex Swirls

Standing beside my fake fireplace
feeling the heat rise, I think of

those welcome grates all over town
where homeless guys curl up with slim blankets,

and backpacks, filled with scraps of life
and small hopes.

Soup Day

It's a day to stay home,
make veggie Wedding Soup,
enjoy nature's red light
as she turns black and white.
The walks are deep in snow.
Main roads scattered with wrecks.
The weatherman is thrilled.
He's missed below zero.

Azaleas, hedges wear
soft, snow crowns. Tree limbs, trunks
are splashed, streaked with whiteness.
Birds, too dumb to fly south,
crowd the chimney ledges
to warm bare feet and dry
feathers slick with wetness.

Those who love shoveling
dig deep for cement, scrape
the quiet peace away.
The sky lightens, brightens
threatens to melt the view.
Already clumps of snow
slide down overgrown yews.

A masked guy trudges by
with red snow blower, spews
white magic into our yards,
covers those cleared front steps.
I hide inside, stir soup,
avoid the season's pain.

Down McArdle

You almost wish she had died
before her wheel touched ice

on the way down McArdle.
She faced the rusty wrought iron,

crossed toward depths Indians shunned.
No leaves to hide the descent

deep, deeper to vertical,
crunching bushes, smacking trees

until it struck the cement.
On her way to church, they said.

Oh, Dear: Deer

Deer used to live on the edge of Edgewood.
Then the Parkway East cut through their homeland.

Their cousins roam the high hills of Green Tree.
One night as I enter the parkway there

a lone doe stands staring at my headlights.
I stop dead and wait for her to move first.

I should have recalled: There's never just one.
The second leaps out of the darkness, strikes

my bright red Toyota hood with one hoof,
sails off into the night, perhaps unhurt,

but it costs me the shakes and a big bill.
I still see that single foot land and leave.

*

One morning on Mount Washington, my door
opens to five deer in the small front yard—

two, snoozing comfortably in the snow,
three stand and look at me quite unalarmed.

How was breakfast? I ask, seeing chomped greens.
They don't get the question. They don't run off.

*

Along the trails Mount Washington cut, chopped
through the woods that wrap around it, we see

a commanding deer watch us from a rise.
He looks in charge, curious about us.

What are we doing walking in his world?
Trying to re-create what we destroyed?

IV
A Neighborhood of Make-Believe

When the G-20 Came to Town

Out in Squirrel Hill, King Whatshisname
whacked my husband's Honda so hard
the doors wouldn't open. He stepped
from his Merc with cell phone in hand,
his heavy accent cleared as he
lied like an expert to the cop.

The Rearview Truth

In the same week I took
the driver safety course,
I killed a squirrel that ran
from between two parked cars
just feet in front of me.
Of course, it *was* Squirrel Hill
where these rascal rodents
run up and down trees
tear across the terrace
retreat to Schenley Park
tightrope walk the fences
appear and disappear
like something almost seen

or maybe imagined.
I didn't brake quickly
enough, then told myself
he made it. In seconds
a sorry whop against
metal, the rearview truth
lay on Beechwood asphalt.
A curve or so later
two little kids emerge
from between two parked cars.
Yes. Lesson learned. I stop.
Mom is putting them in
the road side of the car.

My Gyne Guy

If someone else did this, he'd go to jail.
But my gyne guy knows how to distract.

I'm stripped down to nothing but my red socks.
(Those stirrups never lose the feel of ice.)

I hide under a flimsy hospital gown,
pull the folded sheet across my belly.

He rings for his nurse, a sure eyewitness.
Are you going on vacation this year?

he asks, opening the flowered nightie.
Holland, I say. *My daughter wants to see*

Van Gogh at home and the fields of tulips.
He retreats. *I have a tulip story.*

As he palpates my neck, underarms, breasts,
he tells how his tulips grew from fifteen

to fifteen hundred. Cars stopped to admire.
He moves lower, feels for trouble down there.

One spring, he says, *not one tulip appeared.*
Suddenly his fingers are inside me:

the front, the cold metal hickey, the butt.
The moles did it, he concludes and takes off

the dirty glove, shakes my hand. I forget
my questions, leave them on his ravished lawn.

Sometimes When I'm Curled Up in Bed

with limbs contorted in odd ways,
my mind takes me back to the womb.
Do I remember those dark days
springing from nothing to something?

Floating in warm, wet fluid.
The first to feel my face, my hands
and baby feet. I lick the soft,
live walls that surround and hold me.

So soon I learn that mother loves
garlic, onions, maybe curry.
Ah, the joy of finding the thumb.
The thrill of discovering sweet.

The constant bumpity- bump-bump,
the swishing, rumbling all around.
Far off, the same alto and bass.
I kick to reach their touch and sound.

At first, the glow of red and orange:
early hint of the coming sun.
And then one day, the lids open.
The blur of life outside begins.

For Grace Emily Curran, born Sept. 20, 2011

Beginnings

No baby is born laughing.
Forced from nine months of comfort,

pushed by once cradling muscles,
pulled from the drowsy darkness,

eyes open to too much light.
A whack, the shock of breath,

surprise at life's first lesson:
All beginnings bring an end.

A Living Simile

She looks like she was carved from stone,
the gyne guy told my mother
as I picked my own birthday.
I've felt chiseled ever since
which might explain my rock-hard heart.

Separation

Before they learn how to hurt,
children bash against your gut
tearing free from your body.

As infants, they press the warmth
of life across your chest
uncovering your coldness.

One day, the line between you
breaks. You bleed in places
you cannot name or touch.

Child's Play

At six I ran with a crowd
of my brothers down a walk
between backyard garages.
From the stair top looking down
on an alley, we shouted,

Graham crackers, graham crackers,
at colored kids playing ball.
White crackers, white crackers,
they screamed back. Then we bellowed
the sweet smear again. They edged

toward us. We ran in terror,
our hearts, feet—tripping, pounding.
We taste better than you,
they shrieked from the bottom step.
I couldn't argue with that.

Getting Down and Dirty

I reached the age of reason at six
when Rita Needham squatted beside

a muddy puddle in her side yard.
A four or five-year-old innocent.

Spread that mud on your arms, I urged.
Your legs. Your face. She stopped each time

and asked wide-eyed, *Is it OK?*
She answered a distant call to dinner.

I heard her mother's shrieks, Rita's wail.
My face was as hot as Rita's bottom.

Logic 101

We sit in front of the open door
of his coal furnace. It glows orange
and gold warming us and the basement.

Jockey is as old as my five years
can imagine anyone being.
He tells the scariest stories ever.

We were friends from the two ends of age.
I go to see him in my pj's at sunrise.
His daughter Missy carries me home.

My mother says that nice little girls
don't pay visits in their pajamas.
I wanted to be a nice little girl.

Next morning I remove the offending
nightwear prepared for a proper visit.
Missy brings me home in one of his shirts.

Inclinations

We didn't know a penis
from a platypus.

Two six-year-old girls playing
movie stars on the back porch

of a Pittsburgh apartment house.
Yet, we wrapped ourselves around

those thick, strong straight pillars
and wondered at the carved curves

of Victorian wooden lace hung
like underwear between them.

First Taste

She sat in the dust and heat of August.
A skinny kid snatching ripe Concord grapes

hanging over a wooden trellis
in her neighbor's backyard. She couldn't stop

intoxicated by the flavor bursting
in her mouth from the luscious blue spheres

with just a splash of gray and a promise
of forbidden fruit still to come her way.

To Indovina's

Sometimes, I took a trip up the alley
across Ivy Street to Indovina's.

Mother needed tomatoes for salad.
How much are they? I would ask the lady.

How much do you have? she would ask me.
I think sometimes she won. Sometimes she lost.

My number and her number always matched.

Color Lines in Shadyside

Get that black boy off the front porch,
Gram said when I brought a Thai friend
home from tennis for some iced tea.
I told her Thais are not Negroes
but black skin meant black, she believed.

*

Put more black faces on TV,
our interracial gang had urged.
Apologize, the bishop said.
I gave up Catholic race work then.

*

When my dark Arab date arrived,
my brother teased, *A camel*
just pulled up out front. We all laughed.
That was before 9/11.
No one feared Arabs or Muslims.

*

We're adopting a baby girl,
I told my mother nervously.
Her only question: *What color?*
She was pleased to hear she was pink
but never babysat the kid.

Streetcar Date

I couldn't pick him out of a lineup—
short, older brother of a high-school friend.
Killer blue eyes, a scratchy wool jacket.

I don't remember where we went or why.
There on the last seat of the clanging car
I oozed hormones screaming with desire.

Don't recall what might have made me so hot.
Only know that a lifetime later
I'm grateful he had no borrowed car.

Growing Up with Brothers

Among my siblings who are mostly male
farts were the grandest of jokes. Groucho Marx,

Red Skelton, George Carlin rolled into
one beautiful toot. Mother, Aunt Maggie,

and Gram were too polite to discuss farts,
though Aunt Maggie advised in private

I could *make it go up instead of down.*
David, the favorite, was the star farter

and burper, too. One followed the other
in a dramatic, two-note crescendo.

Suppressed laughter rocked the dinner table.
Why are natural functions so funny?

Just say *penis,* and everyone perks up.
Add a little *fuck,* and they're in your hands.

Sex Education

Maureen Murray bragged about her period—
squishy, ugly, bloody, Kotex-soaking—
all the way home from sixth grade. My body took

two more years to catch up. My mother explained
it all in twenty seconds. Aunt Maggie said,
You'll swing in a hammock like the rest of us.

The Unkindness of Strangers

Betty's face bulge was the worst handicap
in our high school class of near two hundred.

Plenty of others hid among normals:
depressed, afraid, seated in C, D, E.

But her left cheek swelled out like a grapefruit.
She had a mean streak and a need to rule.

One day we walked down Alder together.
A nasty stranger looked at her and said,

Hey, who punched you in the cheek, kiddo?
I felt like I had been slapped in the face.

She didn't answer. *You get used to it,*
she lied. She went to the convent, then left.

Last I heard, she had died on the young side.

Learning to Edit

Second semester, senior year
at Sacred Heart High School for girls.
Editors work on the yearbook,
an early, serious deadline
demanding as a commandment
respected like a commandment.

But damn, every week we are forced
to remove another photo,
shift the slippery layout around
to fit. Someone else is pregnant,
drops out. No diploma for her.
Bad girls don't get pregnant, mother says.

Doesn't mention contraceptives
or aborting the problem away.
Some marry and have the baby.
Some carry and give it away.
Some abort and move on alone.
Now contraceptives have changed lives

for the girls and their parents.
Fewer babies cry over
the baptismal font or show up
for pre-school or kindergarten.
Some couples have puppies instead.
That makes divorce a lot easier.

The Tack Attack

How we tormented that great hulk
of a woman hidden in black
bonnet and habit, head to toe.
Plain, big nose, unsmiling, afraid.
She turned to write on the blackboard

and squeaks arose across the room
like a tin bucket of crickets
with no specific location.
Red-faced she lifted her tack box
and pitched it at the teenage girls.

Stunned, we recovered with laughter,
called it Renaldo's tack attack.
Later we learned she ran away
with the food delivery guy.
She came back after the weekend.

High School Reunion

The girls from Sacred Heart
have barely changed.
They color their hair.
They gain a few pounds.

They laugh at the nuns
except ones they love.
Some married prom dates.
Some single again.

Some are sad widows.
Some have tons of kids.
Some have real careers.
We know each other,

claim we always will.
Later when we see
photos, we wonder
who *are* these old women.

Dear Sister Rosemary,

I've been meaning to write
for most of my life.
The nuns wouldn't let you
answer when you joined them.
The world will forget you,
they said. Made sure it did.

I wrote to a blank wall
for a few months until
college, life intruded,
and you seemed to have died.

You nursed a dying nun
with such joy and kindness
they said you made your choice
between teaching and nursing
when choices were narrow.
You obeyed the order.

I'm proud of your life
and our one-time friendship
as we sat and giggled
in alphabetical order.
You were editor-in-chief
on our tough *Scrivener.*
Sister Mary Agnes
gave me the editorial page.
Always had an opinion.

Wish I'd sent more letters
off to the blessed dark.
Just writing turns on lights.
You don't always need
an answer.

The Dirty Word

Never in my grade school science class,
never in high school biology,
never in college biology
did anyone—lay or nun—mention

The Penis

Mother colluded in this silence
and she with four babies with danglers.
I had to learn about it myself—
this thingamajig on a boy child

and it with a hundred fifty names
from albino cave dweller, boom stick
to wee willy, winkie, yogurt gun.
Not to mention beaver basher, dick,

joystick, lap rocket, longfellow, cock,
peepee, third leg, peter, wee wee, schmuck,
stick shift, wiener or prick. Take your pick
ranging from cute to words with a kick.

Let's be clear about this private part.
It's right up there with the brain and heart.
In fact, any guy will let it be known
the penis has a mind of its own.

What I Learned from Mister Rogers

It's OK to be *that* different.
Wear a sweater at work. It's cool.

Put on your tennis shoes in case
you decide to do jumping jacks.

Add some papier-mâché puppets—
a wise king, a lady something.

Let them talk your words and not theirs.
Feed the effing fish if you must.

Don't work at an impressive desk.
Curl up on the couch. Think big thoughts.

Let people know that you love them.

Home for the Holidays

The long table, stretching across the dining room and
into the living room, is gone. The live-in aunt and
grandmother, source of silent bickering, lasted longer than
statistics allowed, longer than the tensions they produced.
The aunts with fancy pies and uncles with whitened hair,
clogged arteries and a taste for gizzards in their gravy,
slipped away. The once-a-year cousins found their own
families and other long tables. Gone, too, are the gang of
siblings—bickering, giggling, stamping the bell beneath
the table till mother shoveling more mashed potatoes in the
kitchen, reddened and erupted with anger that flowed over
the presents no one liked and the crooked tree glowing
in a safe pink spotlight. The brothers paid the price of a
pound of bacon for breakfast. And that distant jangle
for servants of yesteryear blew away the tidy bandage
hiding the dull, sore facts.

ANN CURRAN

Robbery at the Checkout

I remember the day
I disappeared.

I stood in the checkout
line with my daughter,

twelve, blonde, fresher
than the new produce.

An old man, even
to me, ran his eyes

over her, stole things
she didn't yet own.

Learning Outside the Classroom

Mom! I have twenty-six sisters, our only child proclaims
on the phone from Kent State where she's joined a sorority.
Good grief, I think, this sweet girl is a believer. Shut up
I tell myself, seeing disenchantment in the distance,
half envious of her commitment to a female clique.
I'd joined a sorority my second year—so bloated

with my expanding self, I felt I did them a favor.
But I took the streetcar to school, didn't hang in the dorm.
A fringe member until I sang with the Sigma Lambs
at Duquesne's carnival, and we ran away with first place.
I check out the charming Alpha Phi house at Kent State.
Clothing, shoes, boots, books, knapsacks, pizza boxes fill the floor.

I am no longer jealous of these pleasant little pigs.
The May 4 Massacre occurred before my kid was born.
But Kent teaches her how the Ohio National Guard shot
67 rounds in 13 seconds at unarmed students
protesting the Vietnam war spreading like spilled blood
into Cambodia. Nixon talking draft revival.

A witness heard one girl shout twice: *They didn't have blanks!*
Never mind, a gang trashed Kent the night before and burned down
the ROTC building. News to my daughter and friends.
They giggle, act out the sad tale, shoot with fingers, fall dead
like four dead; nine injured; one paralyzed for life. History.
And they, all too young to believe in their own looming deaths.

V
"Cut Till You Bleed"

The Ukrainian Pianist

For Valentina Lisitsa

The sun glitters on Kaufmann's clock.
A flock of pigeons swirls and swan dives
over forest green Mellon Square.
The Ukrainian pianist
just raised heaven and hell at Heinz Hall.
Arms rise from keys in alleluias.
Head bends low on pianissimo.
She rocks with Rachmaninoff's Concerto No. 2.
The audience erupts in joy.
The strings lift and lower their bows—
over and over they applaud
the blonde in golden gown glowing
like the sun setting on Kaufmann's clock.

How English Ate Italian*

The Mafioso dips a biscuit into his espresso,
eyes the burlesque queen in jeans and stilettos

hears the piano, cello, piccolo spill from the casino
flutter from crescendo to decrescendo when the soprano

with a touch of mysterioso reminds him of the ghetto
where they first landed in America. No cash for concertos,

no money for vino, no boat in the marina, no opera.
With little cash or credit, he becomes a bandit, joins the Mafia.

In pianissimo he tells the padre, who replies, *Ditto.*
He tosses confetti on high, eats minestrone, spaghetti

with mozzarella, zucchini and a bit of tutti- frutti
washes it down with six martinis, shouts, *Bravo! Bravo! Bravo!*

Most of the nouns in this poem came into English from Italian.

Viva La Gourmandine in Larryville

Who knew the Pittsburgh place
where Grandma rests beneath
a broken grave marker
where Stephen Foster wept

where Brenda the Brit rents
to folks who sneak in pets
that Big Easy vets treat—
who knew that hood where monks

chant daily prayers for peace
where I learned golf indoors
where The Cigar Den draws
in smokers to play pool,

lounge on leather couches,
burn tobacco outside
or anywhere inside—
who knew that tired old town

would house blocks of artists
even high-schooler Jake
making safe soy candles,
Guglielmo Botter

whose cemetery sketch
makes you want to book in.
Who knew that burg would land
the *piece de resistance,*

la patisserie—
a real French bakery—
with chocolate éclairs
evil almond croissants,
marquise with crème brulee,
caramel, and yes, "mouse,"
reports one sweet addict
from central Lawrenceville.

Dagwood at the Diner

The French want you to go more than halfway.
They will point to *eau chaud* rather than say
en anglais, Enjoy your green tea, madame.

They will leave *Le Journal de Montreal*
at your hotel door even when they know
you don't speak an effing word of French.

They'll expect you to believe that Dagwood
of the comics talks this lyric lingo
and asks, *Quel est ton special du jour?*

Claes Oldenburg's *Sandwich** at The Carnegie

His *Sandwich* hangs on the   bare museum wall.
brownish crust, near red   like Heinz ketchup.
Left-handed cut cries   chipped, chopped ham.
Cream-colored bread.   Indents of huge fingers.
Meat sits on a lettuce   bed greener than spring.
It's so humongous   we decide to divide it into
twenty thick slices   pizza for those folks who
thrive on wiring,   mesh, plaster, and enamel.

*Not to be confused with his *Giant BLT* soft sculpture.

Old Town Pittsburgh

People could wait all day for a waitress
at the Quo Vadis restaurant, Downtown.
When you did get an order in, you'd hang
so long , you'd suspect they'd called the hash house
down Market Street to handle the request.

No surprise to read in the *Post-Gazette*
that Quo Vadis had found a dead patron
slumped under a booth at dinner time.
His spaghetti *with* hadn't arrived yet.
His boss said, *He never came back from lunch.*

At the Pastoral Musicians Convention

Downstairs at Franktuary, they sell hot dogs
with exotic and mean mustards. While upstairs
in Trinity Cathedral's sancturary,
organist Adam Brakel, with his back turned
to viewers, morphs into a contortionist,
shifting hips and feet, legs right, left and right,
left and right, the whole width of the instrument.
Heads behind him bobble back and forth in time
to the world's toughest exercises for organ.

Meanwhile, over at the Lawrence center
corn-grown Iowan Newman Singers dance
their delight—arms linked, hopping on one leg—
to Joe Mattingly's songs and John Newman's words.
He begs God for light along the *rugged path*.
The singers' joy bobs up like sun on water.

Later, nearly two thousand Christian music makers
rise up, fill their lungs to the fullest and sing
Praise God, from whom all blessings flow....
No one says sing-along twice to these people.
They're choir directors, trumpet players, singers,
pianists, who teach surgeons to use two hands
when they hold your sorry heart in the O.R.

Singing City Rehearsal at The Pete

For Manfred Honek, the ghost; Robert Page,
the genius; and Kevin Maurer, my choir director

Sopranos ignore the tiny man
flailing his arms on stage, commanding sound.
They watch the giant screen where he becomes
a Nordic god in control of their breath.
 Sweet voices arise from the violins,
smushed together like an urban ghetto.
He adds a cello, an oboe or two.
Instruments talk, blend and he hears the harp
when only God and angels know it speaks.
He strikes the match for Verdi's *Dies Irae.*
Singers deliver a karate chop,
ff explosion and scary whispers.
Terror, Page urges. *Catholicism*

at its best guilt trip. Hammer! Staccato!
Honek's left index finger cues the brass.
And then he hears the error: The big screen
runs a second or so behind his hands.
In basketball games that may not matter.
When shushing two thousand voices, it does.
Don't look at the ghost on the screen, he says.
Sopranos tend to ignore suggestions.
The screen darkens. The little guy takes charge,
substitutes a hum for Mahler's German.
Wraps it all, start to finish, in the dream
of Finlandia: hope, understanding, peace.
The hint that all love their lands as we do.

Word from the Rooftop

For Amanda Bruce, director
of liturgical music, St. Mary
of the Mount Church

What the music director taught us: Loud
is not the best our single voice can do.

It can make the lyrics open your heart.
It can ooh and aah up and down your spine.

It can stand tall or shrink to very small.
It can blend sopranos at the rooftop

with earnest altos echoing below.
It can let tenors fly above the pews,

allow basses to thunder under all.
It can arrive at the ears and altar

as one magnificent prayer of sung praise
for the Superstar who invented sound.

At the Temple

The swami looks like Jesus.
Maybe after forty days
in the desert. Shabby beard.
Straggly hair to his shoulders.
Orange robe on a stick figure.
Legs folded flat on his throne,
he tells us God is our breath.
We should follow it: In. Out.
We should raise our arms and chant
whatever name we call God.
We should stretch our hand to foot,
raise arm and eyes to the sky.
Stand like a cross, twist our arms

first to the left, then the right.
We should kneel like a lion,
roar our despair into the air.
We should tickle our partner,
laugh until tears wet our cheeks.
Women in saris find me
a female buddy to spur
the relaxation of laughter.
Swami says treasure your bodies
before we collect our shoes
abandoned at the entrance.
I walk away full of God,
a gleaming tabernacle.

The Two-Headed Turtle

My yoga instructor invites
her favorite yogi master
from India to demonstrate
what a feisty eighty-year-old
can do despite wear and wrinkles.
He sports what looks like a diaper,
shows off his folds once filled with fat.
in a pose I call the turtle.

He tells my teacher to kneel down,
bring her arms and hands to the floor.
He mounts her, boldly creating
a two-headed turtle he holds
forever. She doesn't like it.
His tiny smirk tells me his thoughts.
I still regret not jumping up
and shouting: *Stop! Stop, you bastard!*

Confession

The priest was my former student.
Never noticed the soft green eyes,

the kindness in his boyish face.
But how he argues with my sins!

*Don't think of prayer till I'm in bed.
God doesn't care what time you pray.*

*Make snap judgments about people.
Nah, you probably were right on.*

I wish I had something juicy
to confess, involving my tongue

and someone else's tongue doing
things I can't really go into.

Or tell him I still hate the creep
who stunned me with a first French kiss.

Or admit the roadblock: only
a nodding acquaintance with God.

So I confess my sorry, old sins
to a guy who just won't buy them.

Midmorning at St. Mary of Mercy

Early Mass is over. In a back pew
a disheveled woman appears passed out:

head on chest. A business dude rushes in,
lights his candle, takes a quick-ask pause, leaves.

A scruffy guy heads out for Red Door food.
A devout fashionista strolls the aisle,

kneels at the altar, heads for the statue
of Mary holding a toddler Jesus,

a Pieta thirty years earlier.
She lights her candle, touches the statue,

back to the altar, down the aisle and out.
A woman with thigh-sized upper arms rests

face down on pew but checks out arrivals.
She oozes fast fury, jumps up, right-turns

to the Mary statue, stands, hands on hips,
like she's giving hell to Mary and Son.

Back in her seat, head down again, struggling.
On her second trip, she kneels and clutches

at the altar, proceeds to the statue,
clings to Jesus's foot and Mary's hand.

Dealing with God

Suppose your God is a know-it-all.
Whatever is, or was, or will be
he or she or it knows it inside out.

How do you surprise such a Divine?
I know no more than a bug on a rock.
Perhaps, just showing up when your God

least expects it. Use that free will. Speak up!
Or a better strategy: Listen.
This could surprise almost any god.

A Place in the Sun

The flowers always find their way
to light. Ditch lilies stretch so tall
and then bow to cement and sun

to fire their orange. Some weeds rise
to great heights. A dandelion,
hidden in a hedge, grows two feet

to show off scraggly petals
and raise its seed head to the stars.
And we, rulers of creation,

shy away from the burning sun,
skulk beneath umbrellas, salves, hats
like we were not made for this place.

"Cut Till You Bleed"

Philip Brady in "Ordering the Storm:
How to Put Together a Book of Poems"

I went to sleep slashing my words
as ordered by my last teacher.

If the gingko *dances with wind*
it's chopped off as too romantic.

When *last light kisses Dingle's sea*
with a soft touch, it's time to cut.

When a butterfly tattoo takes flight
with a flutter, my lingo inflates.

When I imitate Joyce with talk
that won't stop, I've overwritten.

When my poem makes people laugh,
I'm cute, self-consciously clever.

When I add up all the critiques
they build one great heap of bullshit.

But: I cut the butterfly flutter,
though I swear I saw that bugger move.

A Chocolate Wall

In the end, the poetry class
ran into a chocolate wall.

Brownies, much more icing than cake,
M&Ms and Hershey kisses

rocketed the poets into
a sugar high, marring judgment.

Forgotten was the black and white
bickering about the right word

to call a former colored kid.
Chocolate was not an option.

No mention of the black woman
who cut out two classes early.

How a Female Poet Gets Published
by a Male Editor

Talk dirty, hon. You must tell
everything and then some. Hell,
if it's not enough, make it up.
Be sure to mention your D-cup.
No detail is too large or small.
Bare your breasts, behind, soul and all.

Have sex anywhere but in a car
or bed—the head at the corner bar,
submerged in a park fountain,
halfway up a green mountain,
in the cereal aisle at Giant Eagle.
Add every detail: the honey, the jiggle.
Throw in some naughty coke or weed
along with the free-flowing seed.

Make the lingo as base as you can:
cock talk and effing like a man.
Get into all the orifices—
whatever your man dreams or wishes.
Convince that male editor
you, too, are a predator.
That, in fact, Erato is your muse.
You'll find fewer poems refused.

The Importance of Being Oscar

Oscar lounges atop a rock
across from the Merrion Square

home of dad, the queen's oculist,
mum, a poet with packed salon.

Ireland remembers its bad boy
in this dark corner of the park.

Awkward sprawl on a big boulder,
reborn in granite, shades of jade

that sparkle on dark pants and shoes,
green smoking jacket with quilted,

scarlet collar and cuffs. A sneer
from the man who makes us all laugh.

What would he think of the U.S.
where he could marry in one state

and get murdered in another?
He'd like the luscious irony,

laugh at inconsistency, note:
the gender-bender just happened.

Love, lust don't always make perfect
or exact anatomical sense.

Undercover and Not

He paints an ugly picture of his life,
undercover and not. Dealt with the dregs.
But when he writes about wrestling with the three
masseuses-cum-prostitutes, it becomes
clear: if you dig in dirt, you get dirty.

Do the Math

My book
Me First
contains
about
nine thou-
sand words:
some sharp
smart-ass
funny
precise
not nice
dilly-
dally
up your
alley.
Some dull
like *a*
and *the*.
A few
damn near
divine.

The book
sells for
fifteen
dollars.
I earn
0.0016922383
cents a word.
Who says
the U.S.
doesn't
value
poets?

A Rough Reading at St. Francis University

Off in the cool Pennsylvania woodlands
at the sleek John F. Kennedy Center,
belatedly blessed by Eunice Shriver,
I see a vast study hall, papers, talk,
turn into a required cultural event—
kids on the left, English profs on the right,
me and my poems on the podium.
This is the smallest Division 1 school,
the lean ex-hoopster, female chaplain says.
The monks across the rural road made marks
on this place. They built Roundstone Cottage

named for the founders' hometown in Ireland,
for two women who cooked their lives away here,
where I will spend a cozy, snowy night.
I try *Domenic's Dictionary* on them.
Some chuckle about censored words—
vagina, penis—left out for fifth graders.
Some suffer through this weird requirement.
A lone black kid, built like ex-Steeler Bettis,
looks like he's suffering from a tough tackle.
He pulls his gray hoodie over his face.
As I launch into *Marking Time and Place,*

a real rant about the wonders of Ireland.
A big, tall guy elbows on knees stares intent,
He looks as though he will tear me apart
if I utter one more green metaphor.
Thank God for the English profs who chuckle
over irony and complexities.
An English major asks about process.
It's all too slip-slop-slash-dash to define—
getting fingers to work the wayward mind.
Despite the long-suffering of the jocks,
I find a lot of kindness in these woods.

The Pittsburgh Poem Is

After Iggy McGovern's *The Irish Poem Is*

a Terrible Towel, a political row, a Cyril Wecht trial
a Steeler nation, an education, a million patients
a Golden Triangle, a neighborhood wrangle, a weeping Angle
a river ride, an ebb tide, an also died
a Catholic church, a pre-flight search, an Aviary perch
a wobbly incline, a coal mine, an ALCOA/BAYER sign
a Fort Duquesne, an Old Main, a touch of Cain
a steel mill, a steep hill, a last will
a Warhol wig, a jazz gig, a river dig
a fair deal, a down-at-the-heel, a Ferris wheel
a Pirate team, a boater's dream, an Isaly's ice cream
a bit smutty, an instant buddy, Silly Putty
a PAT bus, a creative cuss, a medical truss
a maiden aunt, a red-hot rant, a heart transplant
a pizza pie, a white lie, a regular guy
a laundromat, an old hat, a bloody baseball bat
a small town, a prom gown, a Mr. Yuk frown
a Neighborhood of Make-Believe, neighborhoods that make you grieve
a card game, an Auntie Mame, a same-same
a boiled pirogi, a hand-rolled stogie, a miraculous bogie
a Mellon bubble, a share of rubble, a teacher in trouble
a Sid the Kid, a Sophie Masloff bid, once hell without a lid
a jail trail, a rusty rail, a deer-hunter male
a clean-air deception, a lack of perception, an immaculate reception
a Dairy Queen, a too-often Seen, a dead teen
a Cathedral of Learning, a minimum-wage earning, a Hill burning
a Kaufmann's clock, a violent jock, a town in hock
a Bettis bash, a Hines Ward dash, some Rooney cash
a reserved-parking chair, Top-Doc care, a baby mayor
a cool I.C. Light, a bingo night, a brownfield site

a polio shot, a melting pot, a killer caught
a coal barge, a Macy's charge, an XXtra large
a Mario Lemieux, an Irish stew, an empty church pew
a Heinz pickle pin, a seedy has-been, any soccer win
a mini-subway, a traffic delay, a secret gay
a Grandview lark, an Eat N Park, a no-longer dark
a labor fight, a fireworks night, a Romero fright
a Giant Eagle, a bit illegal, a backside wiggle
a billion stairs, a street fair, an occasional bear
a herd of deer, an old-fashioned cheer, a come-hither leer
a friendly face, *The Circular Staircase*, a question of race
a homeless man, a Penguin fan, a smoking ban
a bluegrass band, a legal demand, a threat to expand
a Smiley Face ☺, a public TV place, a Civic Arena erased
a Big Mac, a certain knack, a 9/11 attack
a lot of big hips, a bit of lip, a blooming Phipps
a Perry Como, an Anglican homo, a park to roam, oh!
a Bach Choir, a swinging tire, a campus wired
a Kelly dance school, a Hillman jewel, a closed swimming pool
a Red Door, a Teutonia Mannerchor, a Liberty Avenue whore
a taste more sweet than tart, a town with heart, a first museum of modern art
a senior center, a Do Not Enter, a robot inventor
a Gladys Schmitt, a candle lit, a double hit
a local bar, a battered car, a bridge too far
a Kennywood, a creepy hood, a should-have-stood
a first in nation radio station, movie theater, gas station
a Jonny Gammage, more collateral damage, a Jordan Miles
a dinosaur city, afraid of a ditty, ah, there's the pity
a parking fine, a bottle of wine, a final rhyme

Acknowledgments

Thank you to the editors of publications and Internet sites who have introduced the poems listed below or plan to do so. Gobs of gratitude to Lori Jakiela, Squirrel Hill Poetry Workshop, East End Poets, and my friends and family. Bless them all and the subjects of these poems.

Adanna Literary Journal: A Collection of Contemporary Love Poems: "Night Prayer," 53

Blueline: "Morning Show," 62

Cultural Weekly, www.culturalweekly.com: "Occupational Hazards," 32; "Oh Dear: Deer," 70; "Color Lines in Shadyside," 88

Loyalhanna Review: "Boxed Beach," 4

LUMMOX 2 and 3: "Streetcar Date," 89; "Dagwood at the Diner," 108

New York Times, www.nytimes.com/interactive/projects/your-stories/conversations-on-race: "Child's Play," 82; "Color Lines in Shadyside," 88; "A Chocolate Wall," 121

Pittsburgh Post-Gazette: "Inspiration to Perspiration," 2; "At Fifth and Smithfield," 12; "On Tour in the Great Land," 37; "When the Polar Vortex Swirls," 67; "The Pittsburgh Poem Is," 128

Rune: Robert Morris University Literary Magazine: "Parolee Patter," 18

St. Mary of the Mount Parish Bulletin, www/smomp.org: "Word from the Rooftop," 113

The Pittsburgh Anthology, Belt Publishing: "The Pittsburgh Poem Is," 128

The Strip!: "Viva La Gourmandine in Larryville," 106

Through a Distant Lens: Travel Poems: "Catching the Blues," 24

Uppagus, www.uppagus.com: "The Importance of Being Oscar," 123

U.S.1 Worksheets: "My Gyne Guy," 76; "Logic 101," 84; "To Indovina's," 87

Voices from the Attic, Carlow University: "The Ukrainian Pianist," 104

ANN CURRAN, president and CEO of Curran Ink, is author of *Placement Test* (Editor's Choice, Main Street Rag) and *Me First* (RD Armstrong's LUMMOX Press). She has worked as a backroom bakery slave washing dirty pans and snitching icing, and as a conscientious journalist at the *Pittsburgh Catholic* and *Pittsburgh Post-Gazette.* A film reviewer of the love-to-hate school, she reported on new films and the Pittsburgh Public Theater plays for the *Market Square* tabloid and covered the International Poetry Forum for *The Pittsburgh Press*, providing advance features and reviews of performances. She wrote features for half a dozen *Pittsburgh Magazine* editors. She also taught English as a graduate assistant at Duquesne University, her alma mater, which placed her well below an adjunct professor. She learned grammar teaching remedial English at the Community College of Allegheny County, where she found her favorite, obscene example of passive voice written on a wall on her way to class to teach that cowardly way of talking. For a couple of decades, she edited the prize-winning quarterly *Carnegie Mellon Magazine* at Carnegie Mellon University, while her boss, Don Hale, argued with assorted presidents about why they should not fire her. Otherwise, she plays tennis in four seasons, Shanghai Rum and 500 with chocolate fanatics, works out at the Y, does the laundry, cooks, cleans the toilets and performs other poetic chores. Somehow, she managed to marry a kind, loving man—Ed Wintermantel. They raised the most thoughtful, sweetest daughter imaginable—Cristin Francis Curran Wintermantel. She gave them a fine son-in-law, Christopher Buckley. Ann sings in the choir at St. Mary of the Mount Church and serves on the Parish Pastoral Council.

Made in the USA
Charleston, SC
15 February 2016